99 ½
Animal Jokes, Riddles, & Nonsense

Written and illustrated
by Holly Kowitt

SCHOLASTIC INC.

New York   Toronto   London   Auckland   Sydney

ISBN 0-590-93777-4

12 11 10   1/0

Printed in the U.S.A.   40

First Scholastic printing, November 1996

For Ellen Miles

Starting from Scratch

How do you know that puppies are naughty?
'Cause they're in the doghouse.

What kind of greeting cards do dogs like?
Scratch 'n sniff.

Dog #1: What should I do with this bone?
Dog #2: Let me chew it over for a while...

Can I borrow your copy of *Lassie*?

Yes, but it's dog-eared.

How do dogs get rid of fleas?

They start from scratch.

How does a puppy row a boat?

With a dog paddle.

Why don't dogs like to get on the scale?

Because they hate dog pounds!

Dog #1: Where do fleas go in the winter?
Dog #2: Search me!

What's Moo?

Who was the first animal in space?
The cow that jumped over the moon.

What do you get from a cow in a bad mood?
Sour cream.

What do you call a foolish cow?
Beef jerky.

What do you call a cow who gets all A's?

A cheese whiz.

What do you get from old cows?

Wrinkle cream.

What do you call a cow being punished by his parents?

Grounded beef.

What do cows read at bedtime?

Dairy tales.

What happens to cows who fight?

They get creamed.

Did you hear about the cow who wrote a joke book?

It's udder nonsense.

How's Business?

Cheetah: "Spotty."

Anteater: "It's picking up."

Polar bear: "Not so hot."

Alligator: "I'm swamped."

Pig: "Sow-sow."

Firefly: "It's pretty light."

Skunk: "It stinks."

Hogs and Kisses

Where can ambitious pigs go?
The sty's the limit.

Where do you put baby pigs?
In a play pen.

How do pigs communicate?
Swine language.

What do you call a fashionable pig?

Sty-lish.

What kind of pigs do witches raise?

Wart hogs.

What do pigs relax in?

A ham-mock.

What do friendly pigs become?

Pen pals.

Have You Ever Seen...

a fish bowl?

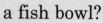

a cat fish?

a dog pound?

a horse fly?

a kitty litter?

an ant elope?

Animals and Computers

What's the difference between a hacker and a beaver?

One logs on, the other is on logs.

Why are computers like sharks?

They both have mega-bytes.

What do fish fear about computers?

Getting caught in the Internet.

What do tigers like about computers?

Getting to go on-lion.

Horsing Around

What do horses tell their kids at night?

Pony tales.

Why did the pony take cough medicine?

He was a little hoarse.

What happened to the mare who broke her leg?

She's in stable condition.

What Do You Get When You Cross...?

...an octopus and a cow?

An animal that can milk itself.

...a giraffe and a rooster?

An animal that wakes up people on the top floor.

...a moose and a ghost?

A Cariboo.

Forest Funnies

What's tall, has antlers, and melts in your mouth?

Chocolate moose.

Why do bears sleep through the winter?

Because they don't own alarm clocks.

Tons of Laughs

What does the weatherman say when it's raining elephants?

"Very heavy showers."

Why do elephants have short tails?

So they don't trip when they Rollerblade!

How did the mouse feel when the elephant insulted him?

Crushed.

What kind of wig do you get an elephant?

A bigwig.

What Do You Want to Be When You Grow Up?

Rabbit: "Bellhop."

Kangaroo: "Bouncer."

Dog: "Carnival barker."

Zebra: "Candy striper."

Duck: "Bill collector."

Second Jobs for Animals

Anteater: vacuum cleaner attachment

Porcupine: backscratcher for an elephant

Squirrel: nutcracker

Giant clam: satellite dish

Roadrunner: portable beeper

Winging It

What do birds like for dessert?
Dove bars.

Why do geese make lousy drivers?
All they do is honk.

WHY STORKS HATE EXERCISE VIDEOS

Today we're going to be doing leg lifts!

Oh no!

What did the duck tell the waitress?

"Just put it on my bill."

What do you get from confused chickens?

Scrambled eggs.

Squid Row

What does a shark look for in a book?

Something he can sink his teeth into.

What do you call a turtle who likes to swim with sharks?

Dinner.

How does an octopus propose?

"I'd like to ask for your hand, hand, hand, hand, hand, hand, hand, hand."

What kind of sandwich does a whale eat?

Peanut butter and jellyfish.

What kind of pictures do turtles take?

Snapshots.

What do rich lobsters wear?

Designer claws.

Don't Worry, Be Hoppy

What kind of music do rabbits like?

Hip-hop.

Was the Easter Bunny always white?

Only his hare dresser knows for sure!

Why is it fun to order rabbit stew?

So you can say, "Waiter, there's a hare in my soup!"

What's Sadder Than a Centipede With Athlete's Foot?

A giraffe with a sore throat.

A porcupine with split ends.

A leopard with chicken pox.

A walrus with a toothache.

A kangaroo whose pocket has been picked.

Animal Talk

What did one bee say to another?
  Buzz off!

What did one fly say to another?
  You bug me.

What did one antelope say to another?
  What's gnu?

What did one frog say to another?
  I toad you so!

43

What did one dog say to another?

I can lick you any time.

What did one leopard say to another?

That hit the spot!

What did one bat say to another?

Hang in there . . .

Beastly Knock-Knocks

Knock-knock.
Who's there?
Koala.
Koala who?
Koala-T knock-knock jokes are hard to find!

Knock-knock.
Who's there?
Aardvark.
Aardvark who?
Aardvark a mile just to tell you a knock-
    knock joke!

Knock-knock.
Who's there?
Dinosaur.
Dinosaur who?
Dinah's sore from telling so many knock-
  knock jokes!

Knock-knock.
Who's there?
Rhino.
Rhino who?
Rhino so many knock-knock jokes, it's
  ridiculous!

Postcards from Animals

"Wish you were hare."
— Peter Rabbit

"Wish ewe were here."
— Mary's little lamb

"Wish gnu were here."
— Mr. Antelope

"Wish you were hair."
— Mr. Tarantula

"Wish you were ear."
— Mr. Elephant

Creepy Crawlies

What kind of reptile tells on his friends?

A tattlesnake.

Why do centipedes make bad dancers?

They have twelve left feet.

How do you bring a frog home from the store?

In a hopping bag.

What does every tarantula wish he had?

A hairy godmother.

Party Animals

What do you call a royal giraffe?

"Your Highness."

Why don't penguins marry?

They get cold feet.

Man: I'd like some coffee for my camel.
Waitress: One hump or two?

How do sheep get to sleep?

They count people.

What do you call a cat who darns socks?

A sewing kit.

What do polar bears like for dessert?

Eskimo Pie.

Is That You, Mom?

What Do Animals Read?

Pig:

The National Oinkquirer

Cow:

The Daily Moos

Leopard:

Spots Illustrated

Cat:

Good Mousekeeping

Dog:

Rolling Bone

How to Insult an Animal

Fish:

Go jump in the lake!

Bear:

Make tracks!

Lice:

Get out of my hair!

Dog:

Bite me!

What Kind of Music Do You Like?

Monkey:

Swing

Elephant:

Heavy metal

Snake:

(W)rap

Whale:

Blues

Porcupine:

Punk

How Mad Were You?

Frog:

"Hopping mad!"

Bull:

"Fighting mad!"

Lobster:

"Boiling mad!"

Wolf:

"Howling mad!"

Firefly:

"Burning mad!"

Half Joke

Knock-knock.
Who's there?
Toad.
Toad who?
Toad you I knew lots of _____ _____
jokes!